TEEN WOLF

Mythology, Bestiary & Herbarium

C.M. DUTKIEWICZ

TEEN WOLF

Mythology, Bestiary & Herbarium

C.M. DUTKIEWICZ

Originaire de Normandie, C.M. est
passionnée de mythologie et aime
étudier son influence sur la société
moderne.

Contents

Introduction

Why is Lycaon the first werewolf? What is a banshee? What is the story of the Beast of Gévaudan? What is the power of wolfsbane?

With over 75 alphabetically ordered entries, this little dictionary, 100% Fan Made, will help you discover the mythological basis that inspired the Teen Wolf series.

Mythology Celtic celtique

Banshee • Black Shuck • Duide • Morrigan
• Nemeton • Sluagh • Wild Hunt

Banshee

She is described as a pretty servant girl in Ireland and an old witch in Scotland. In both cases, she wears a white garment. Her eyes are red from crying. Her appearance and role vary from legend to legend, but she is always associated with death, either as a cause or an omen. The «beneficent» banshee mourns the family members to whom she is attached.

Black Shuck

Black Shuck is the name given to the black dog in East Anglia, England.
The black dog can represent death in Celtic mythology. It is described as a black dog as big as a calf, with curly, shaggy hair and big, bright eyes. It is called «moddey dhoo» or hellhound. The black dog can also be a symbol of hunting and stalking. Dogs are also found as symbols of healing, due to their ability to heal themselves by licking their wounds.

Druid

Druids belonged to a high social class that included bards, poets and soothsayers. They had knowledge of plants and their uses. In Gaul, they acted as educators and performed numerous rites (the only one known to us is that of mistletoe gathering). In Ireland, the druids were all magicians. They evoke the past and foretell the future. They are also healers.

Morrigan

This is the goddess of physical love and death, as well as warrior fury. She is one of the fundamental figures of Celtic and especially Irish mythology.

She is the crow of battle (her functions are similar to those of Athena/Minerve). She is also considered a consort of the Dagda (supreme god).

Her gleaming crew, which is impressive, associates her with the warrior function as well as with the world of the dead. During battles, she undergoes a metamorphosis when invoked, imitating the cry of the crow. Her aspects are multiple: a woman of great beauty or an old hag. She wears red in battle (the color of a warrior): her face, eyebrows, clothes, chariot and (one-legged) horse are all red.

A poet and satirist, she prophesied the coming misfortunes that would bring about the end of the world. Every Samain day (November), the goddess washes herself in the river Unius, where she joins forces with Dagda, enabling him to protect her from her enemies.

The skulls of slain warriors are called «Morrigann's acorns». Perhaps this is why the goddess is also known as the Queen of Ghosts or Spectres. It would seem that Morigane is an ancient form/model of the fairy Morgana.

Nemeton

Nemeton is a Gallic word for a sacred place, a sanctuary. The name was given to a sacred forest in England during the Middle Ages. An oak sanctuary sometimes bears the name Drunemeton. This name was given to several places on the Iberian Peninsula. Nemetona is the goddess of sacred soils in Gaul and Brittany. She was associated with the god Mars in the Gallo-Roman period. Her worshippers were called Nemetes.

Sluagh

Sluagh are Celtic magical beings. They are the spirits of the restless dead. They can approach from all sides except the east. They often appear in the form of a gray bird.

Although they will sometimes rescue a man from the edge of a cliff and carry him from island to island, they avoid mixing with men. They can only be seen after sunset. They sometimes injure livestock when they're unhappy.

Wild Hunt / Chasse infernale

In Celtic mythology, fairies sometimes left their homes and rode wild across the land, snatching people from their homes and taking them away. In Wales, the commander of the infernal hunt is called Gwynn Ap Nudd, King of the Dead. He is accompanied by red molosses called Cwyn Annwn. He rides the storm clouds to collect the souls of the newly deceased and lead them to the afterlife. In Scotland, King Arthur is said to ride the storm clouds in the company of the Infernal Hunt and the Sluaghs.

It's dangerous to watch the Infernal Hunt ride past, except for those who have taken the precaution of placing a rowan branch across their door.

The riders of the infernal hunt are known as Ghost Riders.

German-Scandinavian mythology

Balder - Berserks - Fenris - Frigg - Garmr - Loki - Odin

Balder

Baldr is the son of Odin and Frigg. He is Nanna's husband. His name means luminous, white. Chamomile is his symbolic flower. He is the god of light and beauty. All men and gods love him. With the exception of Loki.

Baldr had a dream that warned him of great danger. He informed Odin and Frigg. To protect him, Frigg made all animate and inanimate beings swear not to harm Baldr. All swore, and Baldr became «invincible». The gods amused themselves by throwing all manner of objects at Baldr, but none harmed him. Annoyed, Loki disguised himself and went to see Nanna in her home and told her about Baldr's invulnerability. Unsuspecting, Nanna told her visitor that there was only one plant (a kind of mistletoe growing next to Valhalla) capable of hurting Baldr because it had not sworn. Loki immediately set off to pick the plant. When he returned to Asgard (home of the gods), he gave the mistletoe branch to Hodr, the only blind god, so that he too could bless Baldr. When Hodr threw the mistletoe at Baldr, Baldr died immediately.

Everyone was very sad. Hermod, a son of Odin and the bravest of them all, offered to fetch Baldr from Hel's kingdom. Hel agreed to return Baldr on condition that all beings mourn his death. Hermod reported Hel's demand to Odin and Frigg, and messages were sent for all to mourn Baldr. All beings mourned Baldr with the exception of the giantess Thokk, who is in reality Loki in disguise. Baldr is thus condemned to remain in Hel's kingdom.

At the Twilight of the Mighty (Ragnarok), Baldr is one of the six survivors who will rebuild the world free of giants and trolls. Balder can be considered the Odin of the new world.

BERSERKS

Berserks were Odin's warriors. Covering themselves in a bear or wolf skin, they entered a trance and acquired the physical abilities of the animal. As a result, they possessed incredible, savage, animal strength. Everyone trembled and was paralyzed with fear when these fabulous warriors appeared. Their power was such that it was almost impossible to kill them, either with fire or with weapons. That's why anyone who managed to do so became more than a hero (like Gumr the murderer).

FENRIS / FENRIR

Fenrir is one of the children of Loki and the giantess Angrboda. He is a giant wolf who has been chained to the earth because he will participate (along with Loki's other children) in the advent of Ragnarok.

The other children Loki had with the giantess Angrboda, who are destined to destroy the Aesir, are Iormungard, the Midgard serpent and the goddess Hel. In order to preserve the Aesir, Iormungard was cast into the sea that surrounds the earth and Hel was locked up in Nifheim, where she takes in those who die of disease and old age.

Loki had a son, Narfi, with his wife Sigyn. Narfi is the father of Nott (Night).

FRIGG

Frigg is the most important of the Aesir goddesses. She is Odin's favorite wife and Balder's mother. She lives in her palace, Fensalir, in Asgard. She knows all about human destiny, but never speaks of it.

When Balder was born, she made all the elements of the world swear not to harm her son. Only mistletoe did not promise anything. Loki used this knowledge to bring about Balder's death. At Balder's funeral, Frigg is escorted by the valkyries and her ravens.

GARMR

Garm is the dog that guards Hel's door. Hel is the mistress of the underworld. Her name means Howler.

During the Twilight of the Mighty, he will confront Tyr and kill each other.

LOKI

Son of Laufey and the giant Farbauti (a couple from the primordial world), he is Sigyn's husband and Nori's (Narfi) father. From his mating with the giantess Angrboda come Fenrir (the terrifying wolf), Iormungand (the Midgard serpent) and Hel (the goddess of the Otherworld). Because a prophecy foretold that these three creatures would annihilate the Aesir, Odin (Alfade) kept them away from the divine territories by throwing Iormungand into the sea, and locked Hel up in Niflheim, where she took in men who had died of old age and disease. The Aesir raise the wolf Fenrir in their home, then bind him to the earth with a powerful bond.

Loki is a handsome god who masters fire and air, as well as the art of seducing gods and men. A «black» deity who creates obstacles to the harmonious course of the world, he is playful and cunning. He uses cunning to bring about Baldr's death, for which he will be punished, but it is also he who offers Odin his spear and prevents the giant master builder from finishing his work in time, saving Freya from marriage.

After Baldr's death, Loki goes into hiding, knowing that the Aesir will punish him. He takes refuge in the mountains, turning into a salmon during the day and returning to his house at night, where he weaves a net. While on his throne, Odin sees him and sends in the Aesir. When Kvasir enters the house, he sees that Loki has thrown the net into the fire and so guesses how to catch Loki, who has metamorphosed and hidden in the river. The Aesir braided a net and threw it into the river, but failed to catch Loki, who hid between two rocks. When the net was thrown a second time, Loki managed to escape. On the third attempt, the Aesir dredged the river while Thor walked in the middle of the current and caught Loki just as he jumped over the net (which remains the three forms of fishing that still exist today in Northern Europe). The Aesir chained Loki in a cave and suspended a snake above him so that its venom would run down his face. Only his wife (Sigyn) remained faithful to him, holding a shell to retain the venom. But when the shell has to be emptied, the venom flows onto Loki, causing him and the earth to tremble.

At the Twilight of the Mighty (Ragnarok), Loki fights with Hemdall and they kill each other.

Odin

The major god of the Scandinavian pantheon, he is associated with creation. With Vili and Vé (his brothers), he creates, from the body of the giantess Ymir (whom they have killed), the sky, the earth, the sea, the mountains, the rivers and everything that exists on earth (trees, stones, lakes). From this, Odin and the gods organize the world.

Odin is the father of the gods (particularly the Aesir) and the father of Men (in the form of Alfadr).

He has a great hall in Asgard from which he sees everything when seated on his throne (Hlidshialf).

He is the Most High, the holder of knowledge, the art of runes and poetry.

He is Rafnagud, the god of ravens, because of the ravens Hugin (knowledge) and Munir (memory) who roam the world and report to him what they see.

When the Vanes killed Mimir (who possesses knowledge of the past), he kept his head, which he wrapped in magic herbs so that he could consult it.

Half the men who die in battle return to him (while the other half return to Freya) and are led to Valhalla by the Valkyries, where they fight and eat the magic boar (Sahmrimnir), which rebuilds itself every morning.

Sleipnir, his eight-legged horse, was born of Loki in mare form when he took the horse away from Asgard's master giant builder (Svadilfoeri). The best and fastest of all horses, it can travel anywhere, including Helheim.

Odin wears the magic ring Draupnir (forged by the dwarf Eitri, who drops eight golden rings every nine nights) and the spear Gungnir (a spear given to Odin by Loki, which cannot be stopped or held when thrown to strike an enemy). When the spear was thrown onto a battlefield, the warriors would soon join Odin (Valhalla).

Mythology Greco-Roman

Actaeon - Apollo - Artemis - Cerberus - Deucalion - Furies - Hercules - Lycaon - Medusa - Oedipus - Orestes - Prometheus - Thalia - Titan - Zeus

Actaeon / Actéon

Actaeon was the grandson of Cadmos. A great hunter, he was often accompanied by his dogs. One day, while the goddess Artemis was bathing, he spied on her. Offended, the goddess turned him into a stag, which Actaeon's dogs devoured.

Apollo

Apollo is the son of Zeus and Leto, twin brothers of Artemis. He was born on the island of Delos, which was dedicated to him.
A solar god, he is called Phébus-Apollon. He is the god of prophecy and divination, the god of the arts, particularly music, healer, guardian of shepherds and friend of wolves. He is as good an archer as Artemis, giving death to men with the gentle arrows of death, while his sister gives it to women.
Aided by Artemis, he avenged his mother of Niobe, who had boasted of having offspring greater than Leto; and pierced the giant Tityos, who had tried to violate Leto. He kills the Delphic serpent, Python, daughter of Gaia who gave oracles, after being trapped by a nymph. And so he had to be purified for having killed a great oracle. He then set up his own oracle in Delphi, where he named his own prophetess Pythia.
God of music, he invented the lute. His favorite instrument is the lyre, which he received from his half-brother Hermes. He helps Heracles, who in turn spreads his cult, as they were both slaves.
Apollo is a beloved god and protector of Troy, giving Priam's children the gift of divination.
However, he is unhappy in love and unable to seduce. Daphne prefers to be transformed into a laurel; Marpessa chooses a mortal, Idas, from Apollo; he grants a favor to the nymph Sinopé if she agrees to succumb to him, she chooses to remain a virgin forever; he offers a thousand years to live to the Sibyl of Cumae

who refuses him, so he doesn't take away the fact of growing old; when Cassandra refuses him, he curses her so that no one will believe the prophecies she delivers.

Artemis / Diana

The goddess of the hunt, sister of Apollo, daughter of Leto and Zeus. Artemis is the virgin goddess of the hunt, protector of animals, children and virginity.
She traverses mountains and forests accompanied by her nymphs. An exemplary archer, she punishes those who seek to harm her mother, and killed most of the children of Niobe, who had boasted of having more children than Leto.
Artemis is a goddess of the Moon, forming with Hecate and Persephone the three phases of the Moon. She severely punished those who forgot to pay her homage.
To the Romans, Diana was Artemis to the Greeks.

Cerberus

Cerberus is Hades' dog, guarding the gateway to the underworld. Born of the union of Typhon and Echidna, he is the brother of the Hydra and the Chimera. His role is to prevent the dead from leaving the Underworld. He lies at the feet of the returning dead, but doesn't like to let the living pass. Orpheus charms him with his music, while the Sybil of Cumae throws him a piece of drugged cake. One of Hercules' tasks is to bring Cerberus back to Mycenae. However, Hercules has to take Cerberus back to the Underworld because his appearance is too frightening.

Deucalion

Deucalion was the son of Prometheus. His wife was Pirrha.
When Zeus decided to destroy mankind for its crimes, Prometheus advised Deucalion and his wife to build a boat (ark) and pile up provisions. When Zeus unleashed a flood on mankind, Deucalion and his wife took refuge in their boat and were spared. When the waters receded, they ran aground on Parnassus. Realizing that they were the last humans on earth, they made an offering to the gods to create a new human race. Hermes, in the form of an oracle, advised them to throw their mother's bones over their shoulders. Deucalion, reluctant to desecrate the dead, finally understood that these were the bones of mother earth. Deucalion and Pirrha gathered stones and threw them as the oracle had instructed. The stones thrown by Deucalion turned into a man, and those thrown by Pirrha into a woman.

Furies / Erinyes

The Furies are the personification of the spirit of vengeance, particularly when a murder has been committed within the family (or among close relations in the broadest sense). They pursue the murderer and strike him mad. There are three of them: Alecto («the implacable»), Mégère («the malicious») and Tisiphoné («the avenger of murder»).
They are either daughters of the night (Nyx) or daughters of the earth (Gaia). When they are not on earth, they dwell in Tartarus, where they inflict their terrible punishment on those condemned there. The Erinyes sometimes accompany Hecate on these wanderings through the cemeteries.
They are called Erinyes by the Greeks and Furies by the Romans.

HERCULES / HERACLES

Son of Zeus and Alcmere. Alcmère was faithful to her husband (Amphitryon). Zeus tried to seduce her, but she refused. Wishing to possess her all the same, Zeus took the guise of Amphitryon and joined Alcmere in her bed. This is how Hercules was conceived. Alcmere gave birth to twins: Hercules (son of Zeus) and Iphicles (son of Amphityon). At his birth, Hera, jealous of Zeus' adventure, placed snakes in Hercules' cradle, but he strangled them. Hercules had many teachers, including Linos, who taught him music. One day, Linos quarreled with Hercules, who in anger brought his lute down on Linos' head, killing him. As punishment, Hercules had to tend Amphitryon's flock near Thebes. As a teenager, Hercules freed the Thebans (inhabitants of Thebes) from the exorbitant tax they had to pay in compensation for the death of the king (Clymenos). To reward him, the king of Thebes offered his daughter Megara to Hercules, who bore him three sons: Thersimaclos, Créintidas and Deicoon. When the king of Thebes died, a usurper took his place and became a tyrant. Hercules killed him. During the victory celebrations, Hera, still jealous of Zeus' affair with Alcmere, struck Hercules with madness, and he killed his sons and his wife. It was this event that gave rise to the twelve labors Hercules must perform to atone for his sin. These are the twelve tasks Hercules must perform:

1. kill the Nemean lion ◉ Hercules strangles it (with his bare hands).

2. Destroy the Hydra of Lerna ◉◉Hercule is helped by his nephew, who burns/cauterizes the base of the heads as Hercules cuts them off.

3. Catch the Erymanthe boar ◉◉Hercule brings it out of its lair and makes it run to wear itself out.

4. Capture the Cerynian hind ◉ Hercules pursues it for a year before finally catching it.

5. Exterminate the birds of Lake Stryphale ◉ Hercules

frightens them off, then shoots his arrows at them (Athena's advice).

6.   Clean out Augias' stables ◎◎ Hercules diverts two rivers to achieve this (in one night).

7.   Capture the bull of Crete ◎◎ Hercules captures the bull with Minos' permission.

8.   Capture Diomedes' mares ◎◎Diomède Feeds human flesh to his mares. Hercules captures them, Diomedes catches up and Hercules feeds Diomedes to the mares, who become docile from that moment on.

9. Taking Hippolyta's belt (Queen of the Amazons) ◎◎Hippolyte falls in love with Hercules and gives him her belt.

10.   Move Geryon's herd of oxen (and bring them to Argos) ◎◎Hercule succeeds in doing so, and accomplishes many feats in the process (including erecting the columns at the Strait of Gibraltar).

11.   Bringing back the golden apples from the Hesperides ◎◎ not knowing where to find them, Hercules suggests Atlas go there, and Hercules temporarily takes Atlas' place to support the celestial vault.

12.   Capture Cerberus ◎◎ Hercules manages to tie Cerberus' legs and pull him out of the underworld, but he has to bring him back in because Cerberus is too frightening.

Hercules went on to perform many other feats and adventures. His last wife was Déjanire. Out of jealousy, she sent him a red tunic (covered in the blood of a centaur), believing it would ensure Hercules' loyalty. When Hercules puts it on, he burns from the inside out. To put an end to it, he has a pyre built and asks his friend Philocterus to light it. Athena then takes him to Olympus, where he receives Hebe as his wife.

Hercules (to the Romans) is called Heracles to the Greeks.

Lycaon

The first werewolf was Lycaon. Prince of Arcadia, he used to sacrifice strangers crossing his state to Jupiter Lycaeus.

One evening, Jupiter presented himself anonymously to Lycaon, who invited him to his table and offered him hospitality for the night. Lycaon wanted to sacrifice Jupiter, but he made sure through a screen that he was not a god. To do so, he had his guest serve him a stew of human meat. A vengeful fire ignited on Jupiter's orders, ravaging the house and transforming Lycaon into a wolf.

He could return to human form after ten years, provided he abstained from human meat.

Medusa

Medusa is the most famous of the Gorgons. The three Gorgons are the daughters of Phorcys and Ceto (marine deities). Their names are Sthéno («strength»), Euryalé («whose area is wide») and Méduse («queen»). They are immortal. However, Athena gave Perseus the power to kill Medusa, because Medusa had boasted that she was more beautiful than Athena. From Medusa's severed head, Pegasus was born. Gorgons are, historically, very beautiful women; but all representations show them as monstrous, with snakes instead of eyes. If you look a Gorgon (and Medusa in particular) in the eye, you'll be turned to stone.

Oedipus

Oedipus is the son of Laios and Jocasta, the royal couple of

Thebes. At his birth, an oracle foretold that Oedipus would kill his father and marry his mother. Laïos gave his son to a shepherd, ordering him to abandon him. Taken with pity, the shepherd entrusted him to another shepherd who gave him to Polybius, king of Corinth. Having no children of his own, the king made Oedipus his heir. Oedipus grew up without knowing his true origins. One day, people at court made fun of Oedipus' origins. Worried, Oedipus went to consult the oracle at Delphi. The Pythia told him that he was destined to kill his father, marry his mother and that his children would only bring misfortune. Still believing that the king and queen of Corinth were his parents, Oedipus decided to leave the region.

Meanwhile, in Thebes, a sphinx was ravaging the region and killing all those who couldn't solve his riddle. Laïos left for Delphi to consult the Pythia. The regency of the kingdom was left to Creon, Jocasta's brother.

Arriving near Thebes, Oedipus quarrels with a chariot that takes up the entire passage. In the ensuing brawl, Oedipus killed all the occupants, except for a servant who managed to escape and return to Thebes.

When Oedipus arrived in Thebes, he found the whole city in mourning, for the king, Laios, had just been killed. King Creon had no descendants, his son having been killed by the Sphinx, so he decreed that whoever succeeded in chasing away the Sphinx (by solving the riddle) would become King of Thebes, and would be granted Jocasta's hand in marriage.

Oedipus solved the riddle, became King of Thebes and married Jocasta.

Several years passed. Oedipus had four children. His two sons are Eteocles and Polynices, while his two daughters are Antigone and Ismene.

When a plague swept through the land, Oedipus went to consult an oracle, who told him it was the people's punishment for the unavenged death of Laios. Around the same time, the king of Corinth died and the people called him to the throne, even though he was not Polybius' real son. Oedipus ordered an investigation, and little by little the truth was uncovered. Jocasta hanged herself, Oedipus gouged out his eyes and went into exile. Only his daughter Antigone remained faithful to him.

ORESTES

Orestes was the son of Agamemnon and Clytemnestra.
When Clytemnestra killed Agamemnon, Electra took her brother Orestes to safety. When he returned to Mycenae years later, he killed Clytemnestra to avenge his father.
The Furies hunted him down and put him on trial. Apollo defended Orestes, and it was Athena who split the debate, acquitting Orestes.

PROMETHEUS

Titan, son of Japet and Themis, his name means «Foreboding».
Knowing that Zeus would lead and win the war against the Titans, he advised them to use cunning, but they scorned him. Prometheus joined Zeus' side.
Prometheus created men from clay, to whom Athena breathed the breath of life. Each of these figures was presented to Zeus. One day, Prometheus failed to present one that was particularly successful and beautiful: an adolescent named Phaenon («Dazzling»). Angered, Zeus sent the boy to heaven and transformed him into a planet: Jupiter.
Seeing that men were evil, Zeus wanted to destroy them and create a better race, so he began to deprive them of fire. Then he wanted to starve them to death, asking them to sacrifice the best meat they could find. Prometheus helped the men: he took a large ox, removed the skin in which he wrapped the best pieces

and covered the bones and entrails with fat, which was appetizing. When the gods and men met, Zeus chose to take the half that was covered in fat. When he discovered the deception, Zeus was very angry.

Since Zeus had deprived mankind of fire, Prometheus stole the fire (either from Olympus or from the forge of Hephaestus) and brought it back to mankind on a fennel branch. One night, Zeus saw that the Earth was covered in flames and guessed that Prometheus had helped mankind; he sent Hephaestus to capture Prometheus and chain him to the mountain. His eagle came every day to devour Prometheus' liver, which was replenished every night. Prometheus asked Zeus to set him free in exchange for an important piece of information: the child Thetis would have would be more powerful than his father. Zeus gave Thetis in marriage to a mortal (Peleus), from whom Achilles was born. Heracles (another name for Hercules), killed the eagle and broke Prometheus' chains. As a reward, Prometheus told Heracles how to finish his work by sending Atlas to fetch the apples of the Hesperides, while he himself took his place supporting the vault of heaven.

Another legend has it that Zeus created the first woman (Prometheus having created only men): Pandora, whom he made very beautiful but with many defects. Pandora was offered to Epimetheus (Prometheus' brother), who accepted her in marriage despite Prometheus' warning.

Prometheus taught men many craft techniques, including metallurgy, but withdrew their knowledge of the future.

Thalia / Thalie

Thalia is one of the Muses. She is the Muse of Comedy.

The Muses are the daughters of Zeus and Mnemosyne (Memory). They are goddesses of the noble arts, music and literature, and later became goddesses of the sciences (history and astronomy, for example). The Muses were of particular importance to poets, who attributed their inspiration to them (stories were originally told orally, so a good memory was essential). Originally, there were three of them: Mélété (Practice), Mnémé (Memory) and Aoedé (Song). Later, there were nine, each with its own function. The muses are associated with Apollo, who as god of music was their master.

The Romans identified the Muses with ancient divinities: the Camenes.

Titan

The Titans are a race of gods born from the union of Ouranos (heaven) and Gaia (earth). There were twelve main titans: Cronos, Rhea, Ocean, Tethys, Japet, Hyperion, Coeos, Crios, Phoebe, Themis, Mnemosyne and Theia.

Some of their children were also considered titans, such as Helios (the sun), Prometheus and Atlas.

The children of Cronos and Rhea are not titans, but Olympians (Zeus and Poseidon, for example).

The Titans reigned when Gaia took revenge on Ouranos by arming Cronos with a sickle that sliced off his genitals and took his place. But Cronos soon became as tyrannical as his father, and Gaia helped Zeus overthrow him. The defeated Titans were sent to Tartarus, where they suffered a thousand torments. Atlas' punishment is to carry the vault of heaven on his shoulders.

Zeus / Jupiter

Zeus is the son of Cronos and Rhea. His mother exchanges him for a stone, which Cronos swallows. He was raised in secret by nymphs in a cave in Lyctos.

As an adult, he formed a plan to free his siblings from their father's womb. He convinced Titanide Metis to add an ingredient to Cronos' drink, which turned out to be an emetic. Cronos spat out Poseidon, Hades, Hera, Demeter and Hestia. The three brothers, aided by the Cyclops and some giants, went to war against the Titans. After ten years, the titans were defeated, and Zeus locked them up in Tartarus (along with the creators who had helped them). Zeus reserved the heavens for himself, Poseidon received the kingdom of the seas and Hades the subterranean realm. Earth and Olympus remained common domains.

Zeus had several wives and mistresses with whom he conceived numerous children (Persephone from Demeter, the Muses from Mnemosyme, Apollo and Artemis from Leto, Hermes from Maia, to name but a few) and Hera (with whom he was married) gave him Ares, Ilithyia and Hebe. Athena emerged from his skull fully grown and armed after he swallowed the oceanid Metis (his first wife). These women aren't always happy to receive favors from the god, who doesn't hesitate to use violence or trickery to achieve his ends.

Zeus is the lord of the gods, acting as arbiter in times of need (for gods and mortals alike), and no one can escape his verdict.

Lightning is his weapon, and thunderstorms are seen as omens or messages from the god.

Zeus is involved in so many myths that it would be impossible to mention them all.

The Romans associate Zeus with Jupiter.

Equivalence of Greek and Roman names quoted in this work:

Greek ๏ Roman
Artemis ๏ Diana
Aphrodite ๏ Venus
Apollo ๏ Phoebus
Ares ๏ Mars
Athena ๏ Minerva
Cronos ๏ Saturn
Demeter ๏ Ceres
Dionysus ๏ Bacchus
Eros ๏ Cupid
Hecate ๏ Trivias
Hades ๏ Pluto
Hebe ๏ Juventas
Hephaestus ๏ Vulcan
Hera ๏ Juno
Heracles ๏ Hercules
Hermes ๏ Mercury
Hestia ๏ Vesta
Moires ๏๏ Parques
Nox ๏ Nyx
Ouranos ๏ Uranus
Pan ๏๏๏ Faunus
Persephone ๏ Persepine
Poseidon ๏ Neptune
Satyr ๏๏ Fauna
Zeus ๏ Jupiter

Plants

Aconite - Armoise - Oak - Mistletoe - Honey - Reishi - Sorb

Obsidian

Aconite

- **PLANT / SUPERSTITION**

Wolfsbane is a poisonous plant. The flowers of aconite napel are blue, those of aconite tue-loup are yellow. Aconitine is extracted from the tubers of monkshood. It is a substance with strong therapeutic properties. Superstition has it that wolfsbane is a poison that can cure fatal snakebites. Wolfsbane is said to be Cerberus' drool that has fallen to the ground.

Aconite is Wolfbane in English.

- **ACONITUM NAPELLUS**

Aconite napel, Jupiter's helmet. Blue flowers

Aconitum lycoctonum subsp. vulparia

Wolfsbane, Venus chariot. Yellow flowers

- **FLOWER LANGUAGE**

In the language of flowers (commonly used in the 19th century), wolfsbane denotes misanthropy or dislike of others.

Mugwort

- **ARTEMISIA VULGARIS**

Mugwort is a plant with superstitious properties (tarragon and wormwood are both wormwoods). A decoction of mugwort made on the fifth day of the fifth month can be used to unbless objects. To ward off evil influences, it's advisable to shoot arrows tipped with mugwort at the four cardinal points on the first day of each year. Mugwort is a plant that represents vigor and brings health to those who wear it. It protects travellers from the sun, wild animals and fatigue. It is a remedy against certain poisons, has purifying properties and helps menstruation flow.

- **FLOWER LANGUAGE**

In the language of flowers (commonly used in the 19th century), mugwort is often associated with regret or bitterness.

Oak

In many mythologies, the oak tree represents the link between heaven (the divine) and earth (mankind). Many sky and thunder deities have oak trees dedicated to them: Zeus in Dodona, Jupiter in Rome, Ramowe in Prussia, Perun among the Slavs. Oaks attract lightning, which is a good omen.
Among the Romans, crowns made from oak trees were known as civic crowns. They are the most illustrious of military decorations and the emblem of imperial clemency.
It is particularly venerated by the Celts, whose tree itself is a temple. The oak symbolizes power and strength (both mental and physical). Its longevity also makes it a symbol of wisdom.

Mistletoe

Mistletoe is a plant with divine properties: it grows and lives without touching the ground. It protects against evil spells, but picking it must be ritualized so as not to sully its properties. A wand adorned with mistletoe can be used to find buried gold.
In Rome, it cured epilepsy and promoted fertility.
The Celts and Germans also considered it a remedy for epilepsy. They also wore it in battle to protect themselves from injury and emerge victorious.
In ancient Greece, mistletoe also had the virtues of a free pass. It enabled Aeneas to pass in front of Charon on his way to the Underworld.

Honey

Honey, like milk, is a food and drink that flows through all the promised lands.

It is the basis of mead, the nectar of immortality in the Celtic Otherworld.

It is also associated with knowledge and wisdom when it is the only food.

Its healing virtues are recognized by the Amerindians and the Chinese. The Greeks used it to purify. Because of its richness, it is sometimes associated with fertility and eroticism.

Reishi

Reishi is an Asian mushroom. It has many virtues. They were known long before the advent of modern medicine.

This mushroom has the ability to tone the body and soothe pain. It is even said to have longevity-enhancing properties.

Sorb

- **Sorbus aucuparia**

Sorb was celebrated by the druids of Ireland, just as the druids of Gaul venerated the oak. It is used as protection against fairies and witches.

The rowan tree has several names in English: Rowan tree, Mountain Ash tree.

Obsidian

Obsidian is a stone found in volcanic regions or on the edge of deserts. Dark green in color, this very hard stone is extremely beautiful when polished.
It was used to make tools before metal replaced it.
Among Central American Indians, it warded off evil spells and warded off evil spirits. In Mexican thought, obsidian represented cold, night and death. Among the Aztecs, obsidian powder was used to cover wounds, as it could both open and close the skin.

Principles found in many mythologies

Demon - Hell - Fountain of Youth - Siren - Witch

Demons

From the Greek daimôn, meaning «genius, divinity». A terrestrial or celestial power, it is an entity found in all ancient mythologies as well as in contemporary religions. Because of their natural strength, demons are often considered dangerous, but they can be positive when mastered, tamed or tamed, as in the case of the Green Giant of Celtic traditions.

In animism, the demon is often the spirit or energy of a river, a tree, a volcano or an incomprehensible or uncontrollable phenomenon.

For the Bible, and in particular the New Testament, demons are the agents of evil, disease and suffering. That's why casting out demons is tantamount to healing and alleviating human suffering. Only prayer and the power of the Lord can triumph over these negative entities in the service of Satan.

Hell

- **Monotheistic mythologies**

This is the place where the souls of the impure and unfaithful departed are tormented as punishment for their evil deeds on Earth.

For the Christian religion, only damned souls end up in Hell, while saints end up directly in Heaven, and sinners must serve their time in Purgatory before entering Paradise.

Hell is Satan's domain, and the symbolism of fire is almost always associated with it.

- **Greek mythology**

This is the realm of the dead, and Hades is its guardian. All the dead end up there. Charon guides the dead across the river Styx to the Underworld, which is guarded by Cerberus (who prevents the dead from leaving). Three judges (Minos, Aeacus and Rhadamanthe) decide where the dead will end their stay. The underworld is made up of several places.

The dead go to the one that corresponds to the life they led on Earth:

- Tartarus (where the wicked end their eternal punishment);
- The Fields of Asphodel (where most of the dead end up, mechanically carrying out the tasks they performed in life);
- The Elysian Fields (a place of delight where deserving souls end up).

▪ SCANDINAVIAN MYTHOLOGY

In Scandinavian mythology, there is no Hell as such. The souls of the dead end up in different places depending on their life. Men who die of old age or illness end up in Hel4's kingdom; fallen combatants end up, half in Odin's Valhalla, the other half in Freyia's abode.

▪ CELTIC MYTHOLOGY

There is no hell in Celtic mythology. Heroes depart for the Otherworld, where peace and abundance reign (like Arthur), while the rest of us mortals are taken by the Ankou5 (a skeleton carrying a scythe and filling his creaking cart with the souls of the dead) across the Great Ocean, westward to the setting sun.

▪ EGYPTIAN MYTHOLOGY

There are no punishments from beyond the grave, but the righteous enjoy an eternal life similar to that which they experienced on earth, while the wicked are doomed to oblivion.

▪ MESOPOTAMIAN MYTHOLOGY

In the depths of the earth lies a Kigallou, surrounded by a sevenfold enclosure. The dead are plunged into thick darkness, their only nourishment being the offerings of the living deposited in the tombs.

The deceased becomes a kind of spirit or ghost. The ghost-spirit, especially after a violent death, sometimes takes on a malevolent aspect and torments the living.

Only newborn babies and those who died before their time enjoy a pleasant afterlife. The unburied have a most oppressive post-mortem existence.

Fountain of youth

The Fountain of Youth is a legendary fountain whose waters restore youth. This myth can be found in several mythologies in different forms.

- **Greco-Roman mythology**

Hebe (Greek) or Juventas (Roman) is the daughter of Zeus and Hera, sister of Ares. She gave eternal youth and immortality to the gods by pouring Ambrosia over them. When she was given in marriage to Heracles (Hercules), Ganymede took her place.

- **Celtic mythology**

The god Dian Cécht is the god of healing. He owns a river whose waters can heal any wound, with the exception of decapitation. His daughter, Airmid, identified all medicinal plants.

- **Alchemy**

The philosopher's stone is the alchemists' fountain of youth. This legendary stone is capable of transmuting matter. It transforms lead into gold and enables man to live outside physical constraints, either by providing the elixir of long life, or by enabling man to rise to another level of consciousness.

- **Legend / History**

In France, as in many other countries, wells, rivers and fountains are reputed to cure illnesses and prolong life. The most famous contemporary legend is that of Juan Ponce de Léon. This 16th-century Spanish explorer believed he had discovered the Fountain of Youth in Florida. The pioneering town of St. Augustine claims to be this fountain of youth. Alexander the Great is said to have set out to conquer the world in the hope of finding a river that would enable him to escape the ravages of time.

Siren / Mermaid

▪ Mythology

Mermaids are present in many mythologies. Their popularly accepted appearance comes from Greek mythology, particularly the Odyssey (Odysseus' mythical voyage): half-female, half-fish, with long hair. They lure sailors with their songs to cause shipwrecks and drown them. The mermaid is also present in Celtic mythology, where she seduces fishermen and lures them to the bottom of the sea. The mermaid still represents the seduction and fatality of the sea.

▪ Language

The siren song: a seductive but dangerous offer.

▪ Fantastic creature

The mermaid is most often depicted in feminine form, half-female, half-fish, living in the sea. Sailors fear her, while landlubbers are fascinated by her. She can be benevolent and the main character of the action (e.g. The Little Mermaid), or evil (like the mermaids encountered by Ulysses on his voyage). It's not uncommon for a mermaid to fall in love with a man and take him to live in her palace under the sea.

Witch

Beings practicing magic can be found in all mythologies and religions. On the other hand, they are considered by society to be either beneficial or evil (depending on the mythology in question). Whatever the case, magical beings are always respected and/or feared.

▪ Celtic mythology

Druids belonged to a high social class that included bards, poets and soothsayers. They had knowledge of plants and their uses. In Gaul, they acted as educators and performed numerous rites (the only one known to us is that of mistletoe gathering). In Ireland, the druids were all magicians. They evoke the past and foretell the future. They were also healers.

- ■ **EGYPTIAN MYTHOLOGY**
Isis is the first of the magicians. She was worshipped throughout Egypt, and her cult was one of the last to disappear. The priests of many cults can be considered sorcerers.

- ■ **GERMAN-SCANDINAVIAN MYTHOLOGY**
Witches are malignant women who torment men by destroying their work and transforming livestock. They travel on the backs of goats, and are often seen crossing the sky.

- ■ **GRECO-ROMAN MYTHOLOGY**
Hecate is the goddess of magic and sorcery. She protects witches and helps them prepare their potions. Circe is a sorceress who transformed Ulysses' companions into pigs when they reached her island. Ulysses was spared her power because he possessed a herb, given to him by Hermes, which protected him from Circe's powers.

- ■ **JUDEO-CHRISTIAN MYTHOLOGY**
Sorcerers are the practitioners of magic, as were the priests of ancient religions. Magic is always black (never white), because it's a manipulation of the world as God created it. Practitioners of magic are almost always women (because women carry original sin and are therefore more prone to temptation than men). Sorcerers and witches have always been condemned and persecuted. The darkest periods have left their mark on history (the Inquisition from the 15th to 18th centuries; the Salem witch trials in 1692...). Witches should not be confused with (king)magi, who were astrological priests who were warned of Christ's birth by a star and followed it to honor his birth.

- ■ **FANTASTIC CREATURE**
Witches are women who practice magic, making potions in cauldrons and casting spells (sometimes with a magic baquette). They sometimes travel on flying broomsticks, and can also metamorphose beings or themselves. They are often feared, but always respected. They can be both beneficial (practicing white magic)

and malefic (practicing black magic). It's not uncommon for a witch practicing white magic to turn to the side of evil following a tragic event. Witches are regularly encountered in the world of fantasy, either as heroes, helpers or enemies.

Other mythologies, symbols and language

Anuk-ite - Aura - Beelzebub - Caleb - Devil - Garuda - Kali - Kitsune - Kitsunebi / Foxfire - Kitsunetsuki - Nagual - Nogitsune - Oni - Satan - Skinwalker - Tezcatlipoca - Wendigo

Ouroboros - Scarab - Triskèle

Alpha - Beta - Damnatio memoriae - Lycanthropy - Omega - Yuki

The scorpion and the frog

Anuk-ite / Anog Ite (Two-Faced Woman)

■ **NATIVE AMERICAN MYTHOLOGY**

In Amerindian mythology, Ite was the beautiful daughter of the First Man and the First Woman. She was the wife of Tate, the wind. After giving birth to quadruplets, she became pregnant again and wanted to replace Hanwi (the Moon) to become the new wife of Wi (the Sun). Skan (the Sky) discovered her intentions and condemned her to live with two heads: one very beautiful, the other grotesquely ugly. That's why today she's known as Anog Ite (Two-faced Woman).

Aura

■ **PARAPSYCHOLOGY**

This is a halo that surrounds everyone, representing the sophistication of the being. This halo is visible only to the initiated, but can be seen by anyone after a direct encounter with a divinity.

Beelzebub

Beelzebub, Lord of the Flies, was originally a Canaanite god. He was worshipped for his power over flies and the fact that he chased them away from the harvest and his temple.
Beelzebub later became one of Satan's many incarnations.

CALEB

- **JUDEO-CHRISTIAN MYTHOLOGY**

Caleb belongs to the tribe of Judah. He is the ancestor of the Calabites. He was one of the twelve men sent by Moses to reconnoiter the Promised Land.

DEVIL / SATAN ...

- **JUDEO-CHRISTIAN MYTHOLOGY**

This is the same entity in literature and visual representations. There is, however, a difference in Christian mythology. Lucifer, the «Bringer of Light», is an archangel who fell in rebellion against God when the latter decided to create mankind. The Devil, the prince of evil, is more a metaphorical entity than a being. But the «real» devil is Satan. Satan is the adversary of God's work. He is the one who tempts Eve in Paradise in the form of a serpent. He is also the one who tempts Jesus Christ in the Gospels. It wasn't until the Middle Ages that Lucifer and Satan became one and the same.

The name Beelzebub is sometimes associated with those of the Devil and Satan. In demonology, Beelzebub is the head of the Infernal Empire, commander of all demons, which effectively makes him Satan. Beelzebub, Lord of the Flies, was originally a Canaanite god. He was revered for his power over flies and the fact that he drove them out of the harvest and his temple.

Satan is depicted with wings (fallen angel), possessing a belt of fire and a trident.

Garuda

- **Hindu mythology**

Garuda is Vishnu's half-virtue, half-man bird. He represents the magic words on whose wings man can be transported from one world to another.

Garuda is the son of Vision (Kashyapa) and Celle-devant-qui-le-savoir-s'incline (Vinata).

Garuda will become the master of snakes thanks to Indra's help. His wife is Progress (Unnati), with whom he has six children. All snake-eating birds are descended from them.

It's an immense bird, huge, strong and aggressive. It has the head of an eagle, a red beak, feathered wings, a broad belly and two arms. Its color is that of molten gold. He is so strong that Indra cannot defeat him. Lightning cannot hurt him.

He steals the ambrosia of the gods to buy the freedom of his mother, imprisoned by the mother of snakes.

Kali

- **Hindu mythology**

The Black Goddess. In Hinduism, Kali is Devi, the terrible manifestation of the destructive power of time, but also the vital force of the earth. As the great goddess of fertility, she is also a goddess of death. She is called Kali when she has two arms, and Bhadrakali when she is represented with several pairs of arms.

Kitsune / Kitsunebi / Kitsinetsuki

- **JAPANESE MYTHOLOGY**

A kitsune is a fox in Japanese. The word designates both the animal and the fantastic creature. For the fantastic creature, we use the term kitsunebi, which literally means «fox-fire». One day, a fisherman spotted a kitsunebi in the distance. He hid in a bush, and when the kitsunebi came within range, he threw down his net. Kitsunebi managed to escape, but the fire remained in the net. It was a small, hitherto unknown ball of fur that burned without being consumed. The fisherman returned home with this little ball of fire. That evening, a messenger from the king arrived to ask the fisherman to go to the palace. The fisherman accompanied the messenger and took the little fireball from the kitsunebi so he could see where they were walking. After a while, the messenger offered to carry the fire, and the fisherman agreed. Then the messenger, thought to be human, took on his true form and left with what belonged to him. When it rains but the sky is clear, it means that a «fox wedding» - kitsuné no yomeiri - is taking place. The kitsunebi has an unnamed cousin (apart from kitsune) who possesses men. These men, who behave strangely, are called kitsunetsuki. There are several ways to free a kitsunetsuki. Make him drink a remedy or force him to leave by locking him in a room with a dog, as the fox fears dogs.

Nogitsune

- **JAPANESE MYTHOLOGY**

The nogitsune is a fox. They tend to be mischievous or even malevolent. Inari kitsunes spend a lot of time rescuing nogitsune victims.

Oni

- **Japanese mythology**

The Oni is a Japanese ogre. He can be found in the form of Onibi and Onikuma.

Onibi is the «fire-ogre», i.e. a will-o'-the-wisp. The Onibi consists of a blue ogre and a red ogre who emerge from the underworld covered in flame. Five or six of them may appear at the edge of cliffs or in cemeteries. They revolve around the beholder. These fires give off no heat.

Onikuma is the «bear ogre», the yokai of an elderly bear. He lives on the mountain and comes down to take away horses or cows. He carries them on his back to the mountains to devour them. Killing a bear brings bad luck, especially if it's Onikuma.

He is depicted with a large mouth and three eyes. He has horns, sharp nails and the ability to fly. He haunts weak people and steals their souls after their death. They often appear in legends to frighten children.

It is said that a woman driven mad by grief or jealousy can become an oni.

Nagual

- **Central American mythology**

Nagual, also known as nahual, is the personal guardian spirit residing in an animal. This belief among Central American Indians can extend to the point where man can transform himself into an animal (his totem). The animal in question is often a bird, a deer or a jaguar.

In some traditions, the nagual is the guardian only of great chiefs. In more widespread traditions, every person has a nagual. It is even said that the first creature to cross the ashes in front of a

baby becomes its child nagual.
Tradition has it that anyone wishing to receive their nagual (as an adult) must find a secluded spot and fall asleep there. It's either during sleep or on awakening that the nagual will appear to the man and become his protective double.

Ouroboros

The ouroboros is the name given to the snake that bites its own tail. It symbolizes a closed evolutionary cycle. It represents movement, but also eternal recommencement.
It can also have another interpretation. It represents the union between the chthonic world, represented by the serpent, and the celestial world, represented by the circle. More broadly, it represents the union of two opposing principles, such as heaven and earth, good and evil, night and day.
For alchemists, the ouroboros, accompanied by the motto «one is all», represents the unity of matter. Matter and spiritual life are in perpetual flux.

Beetle

The scarab as a symbol is primarily of Egyptian origin. It represents the sun's cycle, reborn daily after its death. The scarab amulet is found on mummies, where it symbolizes eternal return.
The ball it pushes carries its seed, from which it will be reborn. This symbolism is also found among Taoists and in China.

Skinwalker

- **Native American mythology**

The skinwalker comes from Navajo tradition. He is a malevolent person with supernatural powers. The skinwalker takes on the appearance of a wolf, coyote or other animal when wearing a skin of that species. Skinwalker literally means skin-walker.

Tezcatlipoca

- **Aztec and Mayan mythology**

The god Tezcatlipoca, god of War and Night, was the protector of vampires and werewolves.

Triskèle

The triskel is a Celtic symbol representing three connected spirals/feet. It represents perpetual motion.

The number three is very important in Celtic mythology. In particular, it represents the cycle of the moon (ascending, full, descending), which in turn represents the mother goddess and her functions (daughter/lover/mother). Three represents the totality of a fact or action (beginning/middle/end), found in life as birth/maturity/death or past/present/future. Three appears in many symbols. The clover is the symbolic and natural representation of three.

Wendigo

- **Native American mythology**

The wendigo is a monstrous creature that eats human flesh. The wendigo was originally a man who transforms as a result of eating human meat. The wendigo is the Amerindian version of the European werewolf.

Language

- **Alpha**

The first letter of the Greek alphabet, it represents the beginning. It can also represent superiority: the dominant male is the alpha of the pack.

- **Beta**

Beta (β in lower case and B in upper case) is the second letter of the Greek alphabet.

- **Damnatio memoriae**

Damnatio = condemnation
Memoriae = memories, remembrance
History
Strictly speaking, damnatio memoriae is a Roman legal act. Voted by the Senate, it consists of literally erasing an individual's name and images from the collective memory after his or her death.

- **Lycanthropy**

Lycanthropy refers to the transformation of a human being into a wolf. Lycanthropes are commonly called werewolves.
For more details, see Lycaon (page 32) and loup-garou (page 69).

- **Omega**

The last letter of the Greek alphabet, it represents the end, destruction.

- **Yuki**

Yuki means snow in Japanese.

The scorpion and the frog

Fable by Jean de la Fontaine.

A scorpion is on the banks of a river and wants to cross, but can't swim. A frog is standing nearby. He asks it to help him. The frog is frightened at first, but the scorpion promises not to hurt him. The frog agrees to take the scorpion on his back and crosses the river. In the middle of the river, the scorpion stings the frog. As she drowns, she asks why he is breaking his promise, leading them both to their doom. The scorpion replies: «I can't help it, it's my nature».

Fantastic creatures

Black Dog - Chimera - Spirit - Ghost - Hell-hound - Hydra - Unicorn - Werewolf - Phantom - Shapeshifter

Black dog

- **Celtic mythology**

The black dog can represent death in Celtic mythology. He is described as a black dog as big as a calf, with curly, shaggy hair and big, bright eyes. It is called «moddey dhoo» or hellhound. The black dog can also be a symbol of hunting and stalking. Dogs are also found as symbols of healing, due to their ability to heal themselves by licking their wounds.

Chimera

- **Greco-Roman mythology**

The chimera is a hybrid monster born of Typhon and Echidna (Echidna's sisters were the Gorgons).
The chimera has the head of a lion, the body of a goat and the tail of a dragon (or snake).
It can spit flames. Belerephon manages to kill the Chimera by attacking it from the sky (by riding Pegasus) and riddling it with arrows.

Hellhound

A Hellhound is a demonic creature of great physical power with the appearance of a dog. The origin of this creature is undoubtedly Cerberus, the dog of Hades who guards the gates of the underworld and prevents the dead from escaping. However, Hellhounds are also found in Celtic mythology in the form of a large black dog, a symbol of death.

Hydra

The hydra is a fantastic creature related to dragons. Its distinctive feature is that it has several heads, and when one is cut off, two grow in its place. Only by cauterizing the wounds do the heads stop growing. This is what Hercules did to defeat the Lernaean hydra in one of his works.

Unicorn

The unicorn is a fantastic animal with the body and head of a horse (sometimes a doe's head) and a single horn in the middle of its forehead. The unicorn is of Indian origin, but its image was quickly adopted in the Greco-Roman world. It was not until the Judeo-Christian era that the unicorn came to symbolize purity and chastity. It is said that to catch a unicorn, a young girl must be alone in the woods, and the unicorn will come and lie at her feet. If the girl is perfectly pure, the unicorn will fall asleep on her lap. However, if the girl is hiding any secrets, she'll be skewered by the horn of the unicorn, which can't stand deception.

As a fabulous animal, the unicorn is one of great power and purity. It cannot be kept in captivity, as it dies of despair very quickly. Its horn is said to possess powerful magical powers. It protects against enchantments and is a powerful antidote to poisons. The term unicorn (French) comes from the Greek monocéros, which gave unicornis in Latin.

Werewolf

A werewolf is a man (or woman) with the ability to transform into a wolf. This is a voluntary transformation if the man has made a pact with the devil.

But a werewolf can also be a man whose nature has been altered by the bite of another werewolf. Popularly, a man is transformed into a wolf on the nights of the full moon (as well as the night before and the night after).

The werewolf is most often a terrifying, evil being.

Some werewolves became so through a pact with the devil.

Some stories make them the natural enemies of vampires.

The werewolf is present in many folklores.

In France, the most famous story comes from the Auvergne. One evening, a lord saw a hunter friend out hunting in the forest. He asked him to bring back the spoils of his hunt, and the hunter agreed. As he entered the forest, he was attacked by a wolf. The wolf almost devoured him, but the hunter managed to cut off the wolf's right forepaw, and the wolf fled. The hunter picked up the leg, put it in his pack and returned to his friend's house. He recounted his adventure to the lord, and when he took the paw out of his bag, it had been transformed into a woman's hand and forearm wearing a golden ring. The lord recognized the ring as his wife's and went to find her. She was standing in front of the fireplace, her arm hidden in her apron. When he presented her arm, the woman confessed she was a werewolf. The lord brought her to justice and she was burned for witchcraft.

- **MYTHOLOGY**

Cf. Lycaon

SHAPESHIFTER

The ability to change appearance is present in many folklores. This characteristic is associated with gods, heroes and fantastic creatures. Witches have the ability to transform themselves or others for revenge.

Ghost, spirit ...

- **GHOST**

Ghosts are one of those beings present in all mythologies. The living fear them and have established numerous rituals to ensure that the deceased do not return in the form of a ghost (Celtic will-o'-the-wisps). Lemurs can be both ghosts and vampires.

- **LEGEND**

The ghost, revenant, spirit, apparition, phantom6, spectre, is the appearance of a deceased person in real or translucent form. The deceased returns in this form, particularly in cases of violent death, to take revenge or be avenged. There are several rituals for getting rid of a ghost, in particular providing a decent burial or obtaining reparation. When a ghost is unable to obtain redress, it haunts the premises and may transform into an evil spirit until someone helps it to obtain justice.

- **ECTOPLASM**

Ectoplasm is the immaterial substance that emerges from a medium's body when he or she enters a trance. This substance, gray to white in color, is not visible when there is too much light. It is an ephemeral phenomenon, as the ectoplasm, which can take the form of the medium's body, returns to the medium's body after a few moments.

- **SPIRIT**

A spirit is the soul of a dead person who lives on Earth.

- **PHANTOM**

Phantom can be a synonym for ghost, spectre or apparition.

- **POLTERGEIST**

A poltergeist is a striking spirit originating in Germany, characterized by its ability to make noise and express its presence by moving objects.

- **SPECTRUM**

A specter is a bodiless substance that appears to frighten people. Spectres are sometimes associated with ghosts.

▪ WRAITH

Wraith refers to an apparition or specter in Celtic folklore (UK).

THE BEAST OF GÉVAUDAN

- **THE FACTS**

Gévaudan is an ancient region of Auvergne. Between June 1764 and June 1767, there were between 90 and 150 victims of beast attacks. The victims were teenagers (boys and girls) and women. The press seized on the story and made such a fuss that the king was obliged to dispatch his best wolf hunters. The first wolf was shot in September 1765 at the Royal Abbey of Les Chazes by François Antoine, harquebus-bearer to the King of France. A second wolf was shot in June 1767 by Jean Chastel, a local boy.

- **RUMORS**

There are many rumors about these historical facts. The nature of the beast itself. It is described as larger than a wolf. We've imagined that it could be a particularly large wolf, a lion, a werewolf or a canine trained to kill. Or a serial killer? The possibility of human involvement has not been ruled out, as some of the victims have been found stripped naked and buried.
According to tradition, the animal killed by Chastel was indeed the Beast of Gévaudan, for after this date, no further deaths were attributed to it.

- **THE MAP**

Carte des Passages de la (ou des)
BETE DU GEVAUDAN
LEGENDE
Passages des 1er et 2e (?) Bêtes 1764-65
Passages de la 2e Bête 1765-67
Passages communs aux deux Bêtes
Villes pour points de repère
Limites de Département
Les chiffres indiquent l'ordre des principaux passages en 1764-65 d'après les ouvrages de Pourcher et de Fabre.
St FLOUR
CANTAL
HAUTE-LOIRE
RUINES
Clavières
Mt MOUCHET
Auvers
53 Venteuges
La Bessière
Sauges
Lorcières
Fayerollette
Chalelles
Marcilhac
Paulhac
Chaulhac
95
Jullanges
14
St Privat
31 Grèze
Nozeirolles
St Just
Albaret Ste Marie
18 39 41
Albaret-le-Comtal
Maurines
32
Le Bacon
Chanaleilles
21
Arzenc
32
37
Le Malzieu
27 Falzet
Terme
Apcher
7 Prunières
17 Fournels
St Juery
42 St Chély
8 Le Rouget
La Fage
La Grazère
St Alban
Chauchailles
10 40
Brion
Rimeize
Le Fau
Buffeyrette
Fontans
Granvals
Aumont
15 13
Javols
Serverette
LOZÈRE
Erinsuéjols
12
Ste Colombe de Peyre
35
30 Les Laubies
Rieutort
La Baume
La Bessière
36 St Amans
Ribennes
20 Rieutort
19 Le Moulhet
CHATEAUNEUF DE RANDON
LANGOGNE
Rocles
6
St Flour 5 de Mercoire
Chaudeyrac
Estrets
Romandre
St Etienne de Lugdarès
LA BASTIDE
Puylaurent
MARVÉJOLS
MENDE
Le Born

Episodes guide

01.01. La Morsure - *Wolf Moon*
— — — — — — — — — — — — — — —LYCANTHROPIE[1] (L); LOUP-GAROU (F);
BEACON HILL (L); LYCAON (GR); ACONIT (P)

01.02. Transformation incontrôlée - *Second Chance at First Line*
— — — — — — — — — — — — — — — — — — ALFA (L); BETA (L)

01.03. L'Appel de la meute - *Pack Mentality*

01.04. 48 heures - *Magic Bullet*

01.05. Le Puma - *The Tell*
— — — — — — — — — — — SATAN (A); LA BÊTE DU GÉVAUDAN (A)

01.06. Pulsations - *Heart Monitor*

01.07. Une nuit au lycée - *Night School*

01.08. L'Emprise de la Lune - *Lunatic*

01.09. L'Alpha - *Wolf's Bane*

01.10. Esprit d'équipe - *Co-Captain*

01.11. Le Bal - *Formality*
— — — — — — — — — — — — — — — — — SHAPESHIFTER (A)

01.12. Code d'honneur - *Code Breaker*

---

1 *Il s'agit de la première apparition dans la série.*

02.01. L'Omega - *Omega*
—————————————————————— LICORNE (F); OMEGA (L)

02.02. La chasse est ouverte - *Shape Shifted*

02.03. Question de pouvoir - *Ice Pick*
—————————————————————————— AURA (A)

02.04. Abomination - *Abomination*

02.05. Meute contre Meute - *Venomous*

02.06. L'Art de la guerre - *Frenemy*

02.07. Sous contrôle - *Restraint*

02.08. L'Imagination et le Savoir - *Raving*
——————————————————— SORCIÈRE (M); SORBIER (A)

02.09. La Lune des vers - *Party Guessed*
———————————————————————— TRISKÈLE (A)

02.10. Furie - *Fury*
————————————— FURIE (GR); ŒDIPE (GR); ORESTES (GR)

02.11. Compte à rebours - *Battlefield*

02.12. Immortels - *Master Plan*

03.01. Plaies ouvertes - *Tattoo*

--DEUCALION (GR)

03.02. Le Risque et la Récompense - *Chaos Rising*

03.03. La Chasse - *Fireflies*

03.04. Prédateur - *Unleashed*

------------------------------GUI (P); KALI (A); DRUIDE (C)

03.05. Tensions - *Frayed*

------------------------------HYDRE (F); HERCULE (GR)

03.06. Motel California - *Motel California*

03.07. Les Guérisseurs - *Currents*

--ESPRIT (F)

03.08. Œil pour œil - *Visionary*

------ THALIA (GR); NEMETON (C); PROMÉTHÉE (GR); TITAN (GR; ZEUS (GR) LE SCORPION ET LA GRENOUILLE (A)

03.09. La Fille qui en savait trop - *The Girl Who Knew TooMuch*

-- BANSHEE (C)

03.10. Laissés pour compte - *The Overlooked*

----------------ODIN (GS); BALDER (GS); FRIGG (GS) ; LOKI (GS)

03.11. Le Nemeton - *Alpha Pact*

03.12. Éclipse lunaire - *Lunar Ellipse*

03.13. Ancrage - *Anchors*

------------------------------------ APOLLON (GR)

03.14. Malia - *More Bad Than Good*

03.15. Musca - *Galvanize*

------------------------------ENFER (A); BELZÉBUTH (A)

03.16. La Marque - *Illuminated*

------------------------------------ KITSUNE (A)

03.17. Doigt d'argent - *Silverfinger*

----------------------- FOXFIRE (A); ONI (A) ; NOGITSUNE (A)

04.01. La Lune sombre - *The Dark Moon*
------------------------------ NAGUAL (A); TEZCATLIPOCA (A)

04.02. 117 - *117*
------------------------------ FONTAINE DE JOUVENCE (M)

04.03. Sourd - *Muted*
--------------------------------------WENDIGO (A)

04.04. Le Bienfaiteur - *The Benefactor*

04.05. Liam - *I.E.D*

04.06. Orphelins - *Orphaned*

04.07. Bien armé - *Weaponized*

04.08. L'heure est venue - *Time of Death*

04.09. Périssable - *Perishable*
------------------------------------ SIRÈNE (M)

04.10. Les Monstres - *Monstrous*

04.11. La Promesse pour la mort - *A Promise to the Dead*
-------------------------- ARTÉMIS (GR); ACTAEON (GR)

04.12. Fumée et Miroirs - *Smoke and Mirrors*
--------------------------------OBSIDIENNE (P)

05.01. Les Créatures de la nuit - *Creatures of the Night*
-------------------------------------- WILD HUNT (C)

05.02. Terreurs nocturnes - *Parasomnia*

05.03. En plein rêve - *Dreamcatchers*

05.04. Phase terminale - *Condition Terminal*
----------------------------GARUDA (A); CHIMÈRE (F)

05.05. Tout un roman - *A Novel Approach*
--SLUAGH (C)

05.06. Le Livre de la mort - *Required Reading*

05.07. Mauvaises Fréquences - *Strange Frequencies*

05.08. Ouroboros - *Ouroboros*
------------------------------- OUROBOROS (A)

05.09. Mensonges par omission - *Lies of Omission*

05.10. Asthme sévère - *Status Asthmaticus*
-----------------------BLACK DOG (F); HELLHOUND (F)

05.11. La Dernière Chimère - *The Last Chimera*
--------------------------------FENRIS (GS)

05.12. Damnatio Memoriae - *Damnatio Memoriae*
----------- SKINWALKER (A) ; DAMNATIO MEMORIAE (L)

05.13. Codominance - *Codominance*

05.14. Le Sabre et l'Esprit - *The Sword and the Spirit*

05.15. Pouvoirs sans limite - *Amplification*

05.16. D'une meute à l'autre - *Lie Ability*

05.17. Menace imminente - *A Credible Threat*
----------- CERBÈRE (GR) ; GARMR (GS) ; BLACK SHUCK (C)

05.18. La Servante du Gévaudan - *The Maid of Gévaudan*

05.19. La Bête de Beacon Hills - *The Beast of Beacon Hills*

05.20. Apothéose - *Apotheosis*

06.01. Souvenir perdu - *Memory Lost*

06.02. Superposition - *Superposition*

06.03. Crépuscule - *Sundowning*

06.04. Reliques - *Relics*

06.05. Silence radio - *Radio Silence*

06.06. Ville fantôme - *Ghosted*
-------------- ARMOISE (P); CALEB (A) ; MIEL (P) ; MORRIGAN (C)

06.07. Sans cœur - *Heartless*
-- FANTÔME (F)

06.08. Guerre éclair - *Blitzkrieg*

06.09. Souviens-toi - *Remember*

06.10. La Dernière Chevauchée - *Riders on the Storm*

06.11. Le Roi des rats - *Said the Spider to the Fly*
-------------------------------------SCARABÉE (A)

06.12. Talent brut - *Raw Talent*

06.13. Les Images fantômes - *After Images*

06.14. Sans visage - *Face-to-Faceless*

06.15. Bras de fer - *Pressure Test*
-----------------------------------ANUK-ITE (A)

06.16. Le Déclencheur - *Triggers*

06.17. Les Loups-garous de Londres - *Werewolves of London*

06.18. Génotype - *Genotype*
------------------------------------MÉDUSE (GR)

06.19. Nuit de cristal - *Broken Glass*

06.20. Carnage ! - *The Wolves of War*

Table des matières

Élément	Mythologie	Page
Enfer	Plusieurs	47
Esprit	Fantastique	71
Fantome	Fantastique	70
Fenris	Germano-scandinave	20
Fontaine de jouvence	Plusieurs	49
Foxfire = kitsunebi	Autre	58
Frigg	Germano-scandinave	21
Furies	Gréco-romaine	29
Garmr	Germano-scandinave	21
Garuda	Autre	57
Gosth riders	Celtique	15
Gui	Plante	42
Hellhound	Fantastique	67
Hercule	Gréco-romaine	30
Hydre	Fantastique	68
Kali	Autre	57
Kitsune	Autre	58
Kitsunetsuki	Autre	58
La Bête du Gévaudan	Gévaudan	72
Le scorpion et la grenouille	Fable	64
Licorne	Fantastique	68
Loki	Germano-scandinave	21
Loup-garou	Fantastique	69
Lycanthropie	Langue	63
Lycaon	Gréco-romaine	32
Méduse	Gréco-romaine	32
Miel	Plante	43
Morrigan	Celtique	14

Élément	Mythologie	Page
Yuki	Langue	63
Zeus	Gréco-romaine	37

Filmographie

Teen Wolf, the complete series, MGM, 2017

BIBLIOGRAPHIE

• *Encyclopédie du fantastique et de l'étrange l'intégrale, B. Bottet, éd. Casterman, 2008*

• *La Mésopotamie,Ascalone E.,éd. Hazan,2006.*

• *Dictionnaire Infernal, J.A.S. Collin de Plancy, éd. Plon, 1863*

• *Dictionnaire Encyclopédique – Édition 2000 ,Collectif,éd. Hachette,1999.*

• *Le petit Larousse des Mythologies du Monde,Collectif,éd. Larousse,2011.*

• *Encyclopédie de la Mythologie,Collectif,éd. le livre séquoia,1962*

• *Petit Larousse des Symboles,Collectif,éd. Larousse,2006.*

• *L'Atlas des civilisations anciennes,Collectif,éd. Atlas,2003.*

• *Mythes et Dieux de l'Inde,Daniélou A.,éd. Flammarion,1992.*

• *Dictionnaire de la Mythologie,Grand M. & Hazl J.,éd. Texto,2010.*

• *A Dictionnary of Celtic Mythology, J. MacKillop, éd. Oxford !reference, 1998*

• *Dictionaire des Yokai, S. Mizuki, édi. Pika, 2015*

• *Dictionnaire de Mythologie Celtique,Persigout J.-P.,éd. Imago,2009.*

• *Dictionnaire des Mythologies,Philibert M.,éd. Maxi-poche Références,1998.*

• *Dictionnaire des Religions ,Thibaud R.-J.,éd. Maxi-poche Références,2000.*

• *Dictionnaire de Mythologie et de Symbolique Celte,Thibaud R.-J.,éd. Devry Poche,1995.*

• *Dictionnaire des noms de divinités, Mathieu-Colas M., 2013.*

• *Who Is Who In The Non-Classical Mythology, Skyes E., éd; Routledge , 2010*

© Editions C.M. Dutkiewicz 27370 St-Didier-des-Bois
Dépôt légal : Febuary 2019 for the French edition
Dépôt légal : June 2023 for the English edition